My Heart Beats

KINGFISHER
NEW YORK

Copyright © Kingfisher 2012
Published in the United States by Kingfisher,
175 Fifth Ave., New York, NY 10010
Kingfisher is an imprint of Macmillan Children's Books, London.
All rights reserved.

Written and designed by Dynamo Ltd.

Distributed in the U.S. and Canada by Macmillan,
175 Fifth Ave., New York, NY 10010

Library of Congress Cataloging-in-Publication data has been applied for.

ISBN 978-0-7534-7009-1

Kingfisher books are available for special promotions and premiums. For details contact:
Special Markets Department, Macmillan, 175 Fifth Ave., New York, NY 10010.

For more information, please visit www.kingfisherbooks.com

Printed in China
9 8 7 6 5 4 3 2 1
1TR/0612/HH/-/140MA

Contents

What is inside me?

Inside your body there are many parts that do different jobs. They work together to help keep you alive and healthy.

Everybody has the same body parts inside them, even though people look different on the outside.

Your body

- As you grow, the body parts inside you grow, too.
- Your body parts are in different places inside your body. For instance, your brain is in your head, and your heart is in your chest.
- The body parts inside you work all the time, without your having to think about them.

Some parts help
you see, hear,
feel, and smell

Your body parts
help you breathe,
move around, and
grow

5

What does my skin do?

Your skin is like a big stretchy bag.
It covers your whole body, protecting
all of your body parts.

Your skin can feel
the things that you
touch. It can also
feel whether you are
warm or cold.

Your skin

- There are tiny body parts called nerves inside your skin. These send messages to your brain about what your skin is feeling.

- Hair grows from your skin and helps keep you warm.

- Your skin is thinnest on your eyelids.

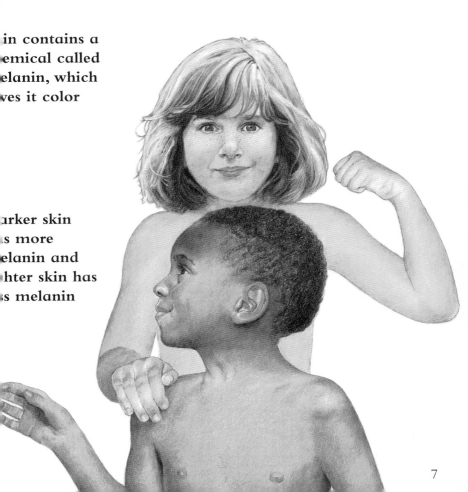

...in contains a
...emical called
...elanin, which
...ves it color

...arker skin
...s more
...elanin and
...hter skin has
...s melanin

7

Why do I breathe?

When you breathe, your body pulls air into your nose and mouth. Air has a gas called oxygen in it, and your body needs oxygen to live.

The air goes down your windpipe into your lungs, where your body takes the oxygen it needs. The gas that it doesn't need comes back up when you breathe out.

Your lungs

- You have two lungs.
- If you fold your arms and breathe in, you can feel your lungs getting bigger as they fill up with air, like balloons do.
- Your lungs work all the time because your body uses oxygen all the time.

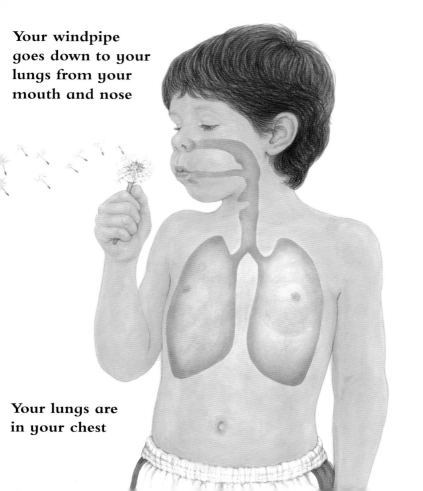

Your windpipe goes down to your lungs from your mouth and nose

Your lungs are in your chest

9

Why does my heart beat?

Your heart beats to pump blood around your body. Your blood carries around the oxygen that your body needs.

One side of your heart pumps blood around your body. The other side of your heart pumps it back to your lungs, to collect more oxygen.

Your heart

- Your heart will grow bigger as you grow bigger.
- The size of your heart is a little bit bigger than the size of your fist.
- You can hear someone's heart beating by listening to his or her chest.

The doctor can listen
to your heartbeat
using a stethoscope

Your heartbeat
is faster when
you exercise

11

What does my stomach do?

Your body uses food to keep you healthy and make you grow. When you swallow food or liquid, it travels down to your stomach.

Your stomach mashes the food into a kind of soup that goes into a long tube called your intestine. From there, useful parts of the food go into your blood, to be taken around your body.

Your stomach

- The food and drink that your body does not need comes out of you when you go to the bathroom.

- It takes a day or two for your food to go through your stomach and intestine.

- You might hear your stomach growling if it is empty. That's the sound of gas moving around inside it.

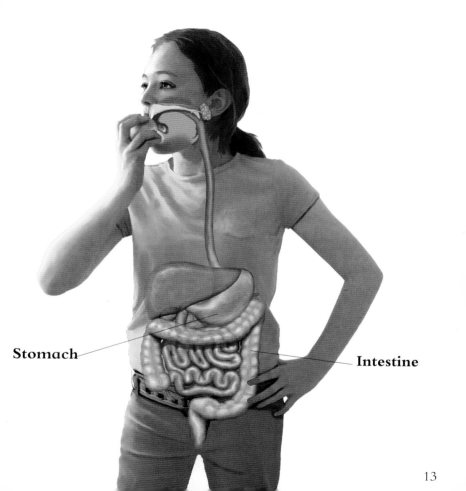

Stomach

Intestine

13

How do I see?

Light bounces off everything around you. Your eyes collect the light and use it to make a picture of what you can see. They send messages about the picture to your brain.

Your eyes make liquid, called tears, to keep themselves from drying up and getting sore.

Your eyes

- You blink thousands of times a day.
- You spread tears over your eyes when you blink.
- Your eyes do not grow—they stay the same size from birth.

our eyelashes
elp stop dust
nd dirt getting
to your eyes.

ou can't see
uch when it's
ark because
our eyes need
ght to work
operly

15

How do I hear things?

Your ears collect sound from the air. The sound travels inside your head to a hidden part of your ear, called your "inner ear."

The sound makes tiny parts of your inner ear wobble, and this tells your ear to send a message to your brain. Your brain can figure out what kind of sound you are hearing.

Your ears

- The tiniest bone in your body is inside your inner ear. It measures about 0.08 in. (2mm) long.

- People's ears can be different shapes, but they all work in the same way.

- Bats have the best hearing of any animal. Their big ears are good at collecting tiny sounds.

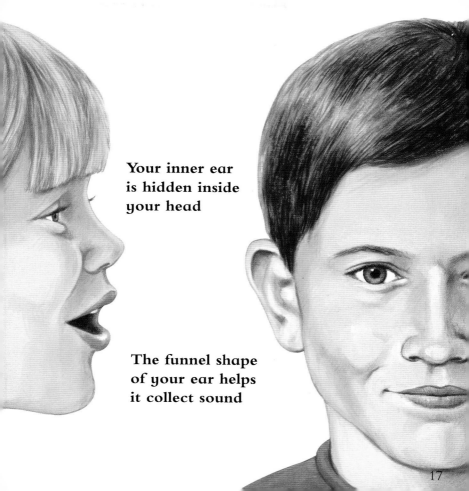

Your inner ear
is hidden inside
your head

The funnel shape
of your ear helps
it collect sound

17

How do I smell things?

Smell floats in the air in tiny pieces called molecules, which are too small to see. Sometimes they float up your nose.

Your nose sends a message to your brain, telling it all about the smell molecules. Your brain can figure out what the smell is from the message.

Your nose

- When a cold blocks up your nose, smell molecules can't get in.

- Tiny hairs inside your nose stop dirt and dust from getting in.

- Your nose makes a sticky liquid called mucus to catch dirt and dust before you breathe it in.

When you sniff
something, you
are collecting its
smell in your nose

19

Why do I need to sleep?

While you are asleep, your body has time to grow and to repair itself.

You breathe more slowly when you are asleep, and your heart beats less quickly.

Sleep facts

- While you are asleep, your brain makes up stories, called dreams.
- You move while you sleep, usually by turning over or by moving your legs and arms.
- Babies sleep most of the time because they are growing very quickly, which tires them out.

**Your body parts
keep working while
you are asleep**

21

What do you know about your body?

You can find all of the answers to these questions in this book.

Can you point to where your lungs are inside your body?

Can you think of a job that your skin does for your body?

What red liquid does your heart pump around your body?

When you swallow food, where in your body does it go?

Can you name a smell that you like, and a smell that you don't like?

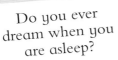

Do you ever dream when you are asleep?

23

Some body words

Intestine A long tube that takes food away from your stomach.

Melanin The chemicals that make the color in your skin.

Molecule A tiny piece of something, too small to see. Your nose collects smell molecules.

Nerve A tiny body part that sends messages to your brain about how your skin—or another part of your body—is feeling.

Oxygen A gas that your body needs to make it work. Oxygen is found in the air that you breathe.

Stethoscope An instrument used by doctors to listen to your heart and your lungs.

Windpipe A tube that runs between your nose and mouth and your lungs.